TOUCHSTONES

Volume B

Texts for Discussion

Selected, translated, and edited
by
Geoffrey Comber
Nicholas Maistrellis
Howard Zeiderman

Copyright © 1992, 1998
48 West Street, Suite 104
Annapolis, MD 21401
www.touchstones.org

First Edition 1992
Second Edition 1999

All rights reserved. No part of this
book may be reproduced in any form
whatsoever without prior consent of the authors.

ISBN 1-878461-51-6

Acknowledgements

We wish to acknowledge the thoughtful and imaginative assistance of Rebecca Dzamov. She added important dimensions of content to the orientation sections and handouts. In addition, she also did much to readapt the Guide's format to make it easier for group leaders both to prepare for and conduct the classes.

We also thank the many teachers and students who over the years have raised questions and made suggestions. This exchange and cooperation is a fitting example of the program itself.

In addition, we would like to thank the following for their help in the publication of this volume:

Boy and Mt. Fuji, by Katsushika Hokusai; courtesy of the Freer Gallery of Art, Smithsonian Institution, Washington, D.C. (Aq. #98.110)

Sloth, by Pieter Bruegel, the elder, 1558, from *The Seven Capital Sins;* courtesy of The National Gallery of Art, Washington, D.C. (Aq. #B-23120)

Random House Inc. for permission to reprint the selection from *The Autobiography of Malcolm X* by Malcolm X, with the assistance of Alex Haley. Copyright © 1964 by Alex Haley and Malcolm X and copyright © 1965 by Alex Haley and Betty Shabazz.

Harper and Bros. for permission to reprint selections from Chapter 3 of *Stride Toward Freedom: A Leader of His People Tells The Montgomery Story*, pp. 423-429 of *A Testament of Hope* copyright ©1986 by Coretta Scott King Executrix of the Estate of Martin Luther King.

Holt, Rinehart, and Winston for permission to reprint "Fire and Ice" by Robert Frost from the Poetry of Robert Frost copyright ©1975 by Lesley Frost Ballantine.

Table of Contents

Introduction ix

1. *The Orientation Class* 1

2. *The Odyssey*
   by Homer 5

3. *On a Certain Blindness in Human Beings*
   by William James 9

4. *Why There Are Children*
   A Tale from Africa (Madagascar) 13

5. *Pensées*
   by Blaise Pascal 15

6. *Stride Toward Freedom*
   by Martin Luther King, Jr. 19

7. *On War*
   by Carl von Clausewitz 23

8. *On Persuasion*
   The Book of Han Tei Tzu 25

9. *Can Lying Be Justified?*
   A Case Study in Medical Ethics 29

10. *Boy and Mt. Fuji*
    by Katsushika Hokusai 31

11. *The Lives of Greeks and Romans*
    by Plutarch 33

12. *Society in America*
    by Harriet Martineau 37

13. *Fire and Ice*
    by Robert Frost 39

14. *The Confessions*
    by St. Augustine 41

15. *On National Education*
    by Mary Wollstonecraft 43

16. *The Autobiography*
    by Charles Darwin 45

17. *On Nature*
    by Lucretius 47

18. *Gorgias*
    by Plato 49

19. *Letter to Her Mother*
    by Amandine Dupin (George Sand) 51

20. *The Autobiography of Malcolm X*
    by Malcolm X 53

21. *Discourse on Method*
    by René Descartes 57

22. *On Arguments*
    by Chuang Tzu 59

23. *On Laziness*
    by Michel de Montaigne 61
    Sloth
    by Pieter Bruegel, the Elder 62

24. *The Way of Righteousness*
    The Sayings of Buddha 65

25. *Selected Articles from the U.S. and U.S.S.R. Constitutions* 69

26. *The Groom's Crimes*
    A Tale from China 73

27. *The Stonecutter*
    A Tale from Japan 75

28. *The Pillow Book*
    by Sei Shongagan 79

29. *The Most Frugal Man in the World*
    A Tale from China 83

30. *A Philosophical Essay on Probabilities*
    by Pierre Simon, Marquis de Laplace 85

Introduction

All of us, teachers and students alike, recognize those moments when a class suddenly comes to life. On those occasions, all our usual classroom habits give way to new and more exciting roles: quiet students speak up with their own ideas, the teachers learn as well as teach, students who often act bored take a genuine interest in what is going on and even take part, students cooperate with each other and encourage one another to learn and share their thoughts.

These moments are exciting, and real learning takes place because everyone in the room is personally and deeply involved in what is happening. But these moments are often accompanied by confusion and a sense of being left up in the air. There is usually no clear conclusion reached and little agreement about anything. The teacher feels irresponsible because the normal classwork is not getting covered. The pressure of next week's test is always present. The students feel puzzled because they are not being guided and taught in the way they expect. Things seem to be on the verge of getting out of hand, and there is a sigh of relief when the situation of an active teacher teaching passive students is restored.

Yet it is those rare exciting times when everyone in the room is involved in learning which we remember as the most important moments in school. We all wish that what happened by chance could happen regularly and more often. Touchstones classes attempt to bring this about. And because Touchstones classes are structured, yet contain a great deal of freedom, there is not the confusion which accompanied discussions when they broke out by chance alone.

Touchstones discussions do more than provide these exciting moments in school. The classes develop skills which students can use in their regular classes, and they create a more responsible attitude towards learning of all kinds. The following are examples of such skills and attitudes:

a. to work with each other regardless of background;
b. to understand what it means to support your opinions with evidence;
c. to take responsibility for your beliefs;
d. to be comfortable when confronted with situations of uncertainty;
e. to respect other people's opinions;
f. to respect yourself; and
g. to listen, analyze and think about problems that do not have complete and simple solutions.

Touchstones Classes and the Texts

Typically, a class in the Touchstones Project has the following parts and shape:

1. Every student has a copy of the text, and the class begins as the students sit in a large circle. The teacher reads the text aloud once or perhaps twice.

2. The students are broken into small groups of 3 to 6, and are given a specific exercise or task to work on cooperatively.

3. The students are brought back to a large circle, and they report or compare the results of their exercise to each other. They then discuss these results.

The main elements of these classes are the need for the students to cooperate with each other, to express opinions clearly and honestly, to listen, to analyze and to synthesize the results for themselves. Competition gives way to collaboration; honesty and openness replace mere cleverness; getting the one right answer yields to developing better opinions with evidence to support them.

Listed below are some of the goals for the students:

1. Learning how to respond to a given text: to modify it, to consider how to apply it to different circumstances, and to take from a text what is valuable for a particular purpose.

2. Learning how to work in small groups to cooperate towards forming a cohesive and coherent response to a text.

3. Learning how to take responsibility for presenting small group results to the whole class, and, in general, to be able to play the role of a thoughtful conduit between small and large groups.

4. Learning how to cooperate in a group of 25-35 students. Students learn to listen to other opinions and share their own.

5. Learning how to distinguish between using a text as an authority (a use common to most other classes) and using the text as a tool for special purposes.

The 30 texts are drawn from a wide variety of authorship—male, female, minorities, other cultures. This variety, in turn, allows and encourages the students to experiment with applying different texts to their specific purposes. The implication of this is that students ask not only "What does the author really mean by this passage?" but also, "How is this text useful to me?"

The Role of the Teacher

The teacher's role in working with the Touchstones Project is noticeably different from the role in regular classes, especially in the whole class discussions. But, since there is much greater emphasis on small group work in this present volume, the teacher's role is generally quite similar to that in regular classes. The main point for teachers to keep foremost in their minds is that in *these* Touchstones classes, they are not imparting information or knowledge, but instead are promoting dispositional and attitudinal changes in the students. This means that teachers should resist the temptation to give background information about authors or cultures and should not praise or correct students with respect to their opinions about the texts. Rather, the proper role is to try to generate those conditions, suggested by the exercises for each of the classes outlined in the teacher's edition, which enhance cooperation among students, help produce fertile uses for the texts, and view serious texts as "friendly." Nevertheless, teachers are still teachers with responsibilities, and discipline problems should be dealt with in whatever manner is usual and effective.

Organization of the Room

Touchstones classes never take place in a room with chairs or desks arranged in the familiar straight line matrix, where most students only see the back of the head of the student in front. Instead, the chairs usually need to be moved at least twice in the course of the period: first, to form a single circle; second, to form groups of three-five; and third, to reform a large circle. Cooperation can only occur when facing the people with whom you are trying to cooperate, whether that is only three or four others or 29. Reasonably accurate circles also make it harder for pairs of students to have side conversations while another student is explaining what he or she believes. Side conversations are a mark of disrespect, and they inhibit the mutual respect Touchstones discussions are trying to foster. Touchstones classes utilize many such devices to instill the mutual respect and self-respect much needed for cooperation. Together, respect and cooperation are major steps towards taking responsibility for teaching others and oneself.

1. *The Orientation Class*

You, your classmates, and your teacher are about to begin a class which differs in some ways from your regular classes. The purpose of this class is to enable you to gain certain skills that will help you profit more from your regular classes. The new class is a discussion class. You will be talking to one another as well as to your teacher. Everyone is familiar with discussions because we have all discussed problems, feelings, opinions, and experiences with friends and relatives all of our lives. However, the discussions you will have in this class differ in some ways from your previous experiences.

Unlike your regular classes, in Touchstones discussion classes

a) everyone sits in a circle;
b) the teacher is a member of the group and will help, but isn't an authority with the correct answers;
c) there is no hand raising, instead everyone will learn how to run the discussion; and
d) there is no preparation.

Unlike discussions which happen outside of class with friends and relatives, in Touchstones classes

    a) discussions involve everyone in the class, your friends as well as students you don't know very well;

    b) discussions are about readings from the Touchstones book and not just our own concerns and experiences; and

    c) discussions occur once a week at a scheduled time, begin with a question asked by the teacher, and end when the teacher decides or when the bell rings.

Because of these differences, everyone must follow certain Ground Rules.

GROUND RULES

1. READ THE TEXT CAREFULLY. In Touchstones discussions your opinions are important, but these opinions are your thoughts about the text.

2. LISTEN TO WHAT OTHERS SAY AND DON'T INTERRUPT. A discussion cannot occur if you don't listen carefully to what people say.

3. SPEAK CLEARLY. For others to respond to your opinions, everyone must be able to hear and understand you.

4. GIVE OTHERS YOUR RESPECT. A discussion is a cooperative exchange of ideas and not an argument or a debate. You may become excited and wish to share your ideas, but don't talk privately to your neighbor. In a Touchstones class, you will talk publicly to the whole class.

GOALS: WHAT YOU CAN GAIN FROM TOUCHSTONES DISCUSSION CLASSES

You will learn to
- a) listen better to what others say,
- b) explain your own ideas,
- c) speak and work with others whether you know them or not,
- d) receive correction and criticism from others,
- e) ask about what you don't understand,
- f) admit when you're wrong,
- g) think about questions for which the answers are uncertain,
- h) learn from others,
- i) teach others,
- j) teach yourself, and
- k) become more aware of how others see you.

2. The Odyssey
by Homer

Odysseus, the great warrior, went with the Greek armies to Troy to fight the Trojans and left his wife Penelope and his new born son Telemachus. After ten years of war, the Greeks defeated their enemies and many warriors returned home. However, Odysseus was not heard from. For another ten years, his wife waited for news while many men came to ask to marry her. For years, these men came to her palace, ate her food, and drank her wine and tried to force her to choose among them. Suddenly, after twenty years, Odysseus returned disguised as a beggar and killed all the suitors. Penelope, told by her son and servants that her husband had returned dressed in rags, came down from her room to see the man she had not seen in twenty years.

She saw the man leaning against a pillar, his eyes looking downward, waiting. For a long time she sat across the hall gazing at him. Sometimes the stranger looked like her husband of twenty years ago, sometimes she could only see the rags he wore covered with her suitors' blood. Finally, her son Telemachus spoke. "Mother, don't you feel anything?

You haven't seen him in twenty years and do you run to him, talk to him, ask him questions? No, you hold back. How can you be so cold and hard?"

"I'm stunned, my child. I can't keep my eyes on him or speak to him. If he really is your father, we'll know one another. There are secrets only he and I know."

A smile crossed the face of the stranger. "Let your mother test me when she wishes. The rags I wear and the blood I'm covered with make her doubt me."

When they were alone, the stranger moved a chair to face Penelope. "You're a strange woman, a hard woman. Who else would hold back when her husband returns after twenty years? Have the servants make up a bed for me somewhere. Your heart is iron."

"I'm not hard or proud. I remember how you—he rather—looked twenty years ago and how he was." She called to a servant and said, "Make up a bed for him outside the room my husband built with his own hands. Take the bed my husband made and move it there."

With these remarks she pushed him to the edge. He turned on her in a rage. "Woman, who dared move my bed? No one would know how unless you told him. That was our vow, our secret. I built the bed right into the tree." He was shaking as he spoke. "You betrayed me. The trunk of an old olive tree grew like a pillar. I built our bedroom around it. I shaped the trunk, drilled holes in it. The trunk was our bed post. No one could move it unless you let him cut the tree. That was our sign."

She cried as she heard him speak in this rage. Through her tears she spoke, "Forgive me, I couldn't love you at first. I had to protect myself. For years I've had to arm myself against strangers, against men who wanted me. But no one has ever seen our bed. When you replied to me as you did, I knew you were really Odysseus my husband, and I am your own." The ache in Odysseus' heart moved to his eyes and he cried. He longed for her as a swimmer whose ship has gone down longs for the beach, and he held her in his arms.

3. *On a Certain Blindness in Human Beings* by **William James**

Our judgements about the value of things depend on the feelings which those things arouse in us. When we judge that a thing is precious, this is because our ideas about it are connected with our feelings. If we were completely without feelings, or if we only had thoughts about things, we would lose all our likes and dislikes. We would be unable to say that one experience in life was more valuable or significant than another.

The blindness in human beings is the blindness we all have about people different from ourselves. Let me give you a personal example of the kind each of us experiences daily.

Some years ago I was travelling in the mountains of North Carolina. I passed by a large number of small valleys that had been recently cleared and planted with crops. They seemed very ugly to me. In each case, the settler had cut down the smaller trees and left the burnt stumps standing. He had also cut away the bark all around the trunks of larger trees so that they would die; then they would not cast shade. He had then built a log cabin plastered with clay and set up a zig-zag rail fence around this scene of destruction to keep the pigs and cattle out. Finally he had planted corn in the spaces between the trees and stumps. He lived there with his wife and children. His only possessions were an axe, a gun, and some pots and pans.

The forest had been destroyed. What had replaced it was horrible—a kind of open wound with no beauty of its own to replace nature's beauty.

Then I said to the mountaineer who was driving me, "What sort of people are they who have to make these new clearings?" "People like us," he replied. "Why, we ain't happy here, unless we are getting one of these valleys under cultivation." I instantly felt I had been losing the point of the situation. Because these clearings looked ugly to me, I thought that those men whose strong arms had cleared them could tell no other story. But when *they* looked on those ugly stumps they thought of personal victory. The cabin was a guarantee of safety for themselves and their families. In short, the clearing, which to me was only an ugly picture, was a symbol of duty, struggle, and success to them.

I had been blind to the beauty of their conditions as they would have been to mine if they could have peeked in my office at Harvard University.

4. *Why There Are Children*
A Tale from Africa (Madagascar)

When the Lord made the world and the universe, he lived with the first man and woman. One day, before he was to send them out into the world, he asked them how they wished to live their lives and how they wished to die. Having no experience of the world, they were confused by his question.

"We don't understand your question. We are always with you and never change," they said. "This has all been like a dream."

He said, "You must go forth into the world, and in the world everything changes. However, before I send you forth, I will tell you your choices. In the world everyone must make choices. You will choose for yourselves how you will live and die. Things in the world change in two ways. Some things change like the moon does and some change the way fruit changes."

The couple was confused by the answer and asked their Lord to say what he meant. He explained, "The moon changes from day to day. At the start of the month it is large, and day by day it grows smaller and thinner. After four weeks, it vanishes and is no more. But then it comes back to life just as large as it was. Then once again it becomes smaller just as in the month before. The fruit changes in a different way. Starting as a seed or shoot, the fruit grows until it reaches a certain size. It remains that way for a while and then, unless it is eaten, falls from the tree and begins to rot. However, inside the fruit are more seeds. These seeds in their turn will become fruit. These are the ways things change in the world. This is how things live and die. Which do you choose?"

The couple thought for a long time before making a choice. If they chose to be like the moon, they could live forever. However, they would be very lonely. There would be no one to help them in their work—no one for whom to care and hope. Their lives would go on forever but they would be the same, month after month. If they chose to be like the fruit, their lives would be short but they would have children to care for and love. Finally, they decided to be like the fruit, and they prayed to their Lord for children. Since that time, human beings remain on the earth only a short time but their children live on after them.

5. *Pensées*
by Blaise Pascal

The Bet

Is there a God or isn't there a God? Which shall we choose? Our thinking cannot come to any decision. But we must make a choice. It's like playing a game with a coin where either heads or tails will turn up. Which shall we bet on? "Perhaps it's better not to bet at all in a case like this when you don't know anything either way." But, you have to bet. You don't have any choice. How you live your life will depend on whether or not you think God exists. You are betting your life. So the only question is which to bet on. You must consider what you will gain in each case and what you will lose. Two things are important to us—knowing things and being happy. And there are two things we all try to avoid—making mistakes and being miserable. Since we cannot know whether or not there is a God, being right or making an error doesn't enter into the picture. We then have to decide whether the happiness or misery we would get if we believed one way or the other helps us choose how to bet. If we bet that there is a God and we're right, we win everything. If we're wrong, how much do we lose? Nothing much! So without any hesitation we should bet that God exists. But perhaps we should look at this more carefully.

There is an equal chance of being right in either case. So if one of the bets gained me two lives if I won and cost me only one life if I lost, I might very well bet on that. If I could win three lives and risk only one, I'd be silly not to risk one life to win three, since I must bet one way or the other. But there is an eternity, an infinity of lives and happiness, if I bet there is a God and I turn out to be right. Look at it this way. Imagine you are playing a game and you must make a bet. There are infinitely many possible choices to bet on. In every case except one, you would win only the amount you bet. In one case, you would win twice as much. Clearly that's the one you should bet on. However, in our situation there are only two choices and not infinitely many. God either exists or he doesn't exist. What you are betting is how you will live your life. If you bet that he doesn't exist and you are right, you win one life. If you bet he does exist and live your life as a believer and you are right, you win infinitely many happy lives. If people can know any truth, it is this one. If you are in a game where you must bet a finite amount of something, money for example, and each choice is equally possible and one choice will pay you back infinitely, you would be a fool not to choose that bet. Because of this truth about betting, we should believe that God exists.

6. *Stride Toward Freedom*
by Martin Luther King, Jr.

[On December 1, 1955, Mrs. Rosa Parks was arrested in Montgomery, Alabama. Her crime was that she refused to stand and give up her seat on a bus to a white passenger.]

Early Friday morning, December 2nd, E.D. Nixon called me. I listened, deeply shocked, as he described the humiliating incident. "We have taken this type of thing too long already," Nixon concluded, his voice trembling. "I feel that the time has come to boycott the buses."

I agreed at once that some protest was necessary, and that the boycott method would be an effective one.

After a heavy day of work, I went home late Sunday afternoon and sat down to read the morning paper. There was a long article on the proposed boycott. Implicit throughout the article, I noticed, was the idea that the Negroes were preparing to use the same approach to their problem as the White Citizens Councils used. This suggested parallel had serious implications. Their methods were the methods of open and covert terror, brutal intimidation, and threats of starvation to Negro men, women, and children. They took open economic reprisals against whites who dared to protest their defiance of the law, and the aim of their boycotts was not merely to impress their victims but to destroy them if possible.

Disturbed by the fact that our pending action was being equated with the boycott methods of the White Citizens Councils, I was forced for the first time to think seriously on the nature of the boycott. Up to this time I had uncritically accepted this method as our best course of action. Now certain doubts began to bother me. Were we following an ethical course of action? Is the boycott method basically unchristian? Isn't it a negative approach to the solution of a problem? Is it true that we would be following the course of some of the White Citizens Councils? Even if lasting practical results came from such a boycott, would immoral means justify moral ends? Each of these questions demanded honest answers.

I had to recognize that the boycott method could be used to unethical and unchristian ends. I had to concede, further, that this was the method used so often by the White Citizens Councils to deprive many Negroes, as well as white persons of good will, of the basic necessities of life. But certainly, I said to myself, our pending actions could not be interpreted in this light. Our purposes were altogether different. We would use this method to give birth to justice and freedom, and also to urge men to comply with the law of the land; the White Citizens Councils used it to perpetuate the reign of injustice and human servitude and urged men to defy the law of the land. I reasoned, therefore, that the word "boycott" was really a misnomer for our proposed action. A boycott suggests an economic squeeze, leaving one bogged down in the negative. But we were concerned with the positive. Our concern would not be to put the bus company out of business, but to put justice in business.

As I thought further, I came to see that what we were really doing was withdrawing our cooperation from an evil system, rather than merely withdrawing our economic support from the bus company. The bus company, being an external expression of the system, would naturally suffer, but the basic aim was to refuse to cooperate with evil.

Something began to say to me, "He who passively accepts evil is as much involved in it as he who helps to perpetuate it. He who accepts evil without protesting against it is really cooperating with it." When oppressed people willingly accept their oppression, they only serve to give the oppressor a convenient justification for his acts. Often the oppressor goes along unaware of the evil involved in his oppression so long as the oppressed accepts it. So, in order to be true to one's conscience and true to God, a righteous man has no alternative but to refuse to cooperate with an evil system. This, I felt, was the nature of our action. From this moment on, I conceived of our movement as an act of massive noncooperation...

7. *On War*
by Carl von Clausewitz

War is nothing but a duel fought on a large scale. Imagine two wrestlers. Each tries by physical force to compel the other to give in to his will. Each tries to throw his opponent and make him unable to continue to resist. War is similar. It is an act of violence intended to compel our opponent to fulfill our will. In order to achieve this goal fully, the enemy must be disarmed. So this becomes the object of War.

Some people imagine there is a skillful way of disarming and overcoming an enemy without causing much bloodshed. However, this is an error which must be eliminated. In actions as dangerous as War, errors which come from kind and decent feelings are the worst. The nation which uses force without considering the bloodshed involved will win if their enemy does not do the same. This is how War must be viewed. To avoid seeing the real nature of War because it is horrible does not help achieve one's interest. Self-imposed limits, called *International Laws,* do not essentially change its nature. They do not introduce any moderation into War. If civilized nations do not put prisoners to death or destroy cities, this is not because we civilized nations are more moderate than other nations. Rather, our intelligence has taught us more effective ways to use force than these acts of mere instinct. The invention of gunpowder and the constant improvement of weapons show that the destruction of the enemy, which is the essence of War, is in no way changed through the progress of civilization.

War always begins in a particular political situation and has a political goal. Politics and the normal relations between countries are not different in kind from War. War is not an isolated activity, it is a tool of political life. It is a continuation of political relations. It simply carries out the same goals by other means. War is just another means of expression for political thoughts. The political point of view drops out only in Wars of life and death between countries—Wars which are fought from pure hatred. In all other cases, the military point of view is secondary to the political point of view.

8. *On Persuasion*
The Book of Han Tei Tzu

Imagine the ruler of a country or the leader of a group and think about how you might go about persuading him of something. The difficulties you would face would not come from your lack of knowledge or your lack of courage or because your ideas weren't clear. The problem would be in knowing the ruler's heart so you could make your words suitable.

If the ruler seeks great wealth and you talk about eternal fame, he will think you know nothing about the world. If he secretly wants great wealth and yet openly talks about eternal fame and you praise fame, he will accept your words but keep you distant. If you praise wealth, he will secretly follow your advice but publicly denounce you.

If you try to convince him to do what he can't do, you are in danger. If you try to stop him from doing what he can't stop doing, you are in danger. When a ruler speaks openly about one action but plans something else and you know, you're in danger. If the ruler presents someone else's plans as his own and you know, you're in danger.

If you talk to him about great men, he'll think you're pointing out his faults. If you talk about common people, he'll think you're showing off. If you praise what he loves, he'll think you want a favor. If you praise what he hates, he'll think you're testing him. If you use simple words, he'll think you're stupid. If you use fancy words, he'll think you're superficial. If you omit details, he'll think you're cowardly and incomplete. If you bring up too many examples, he'll think you're arrogant. These are the difficulties you face when you try to persuade a powerful ruler.

Your task, if you want to persuade him, is to reinforce what makes him proud and hide what he is ashamed of. If he has an urgent private need, encourage him under the name of public justice. If he has an ambitious project in mind but his ability isn't up to it, list its disadvantages and faults and praise his failure to achieve it. If you want to persuade him about a specific action, first describe it as a glorious cause and then suggest that it also agrees with his private interest. Praise men who do the same things he does. When talking about people with the same faults he has, always show how harmless these faults are. If he makes much of his own strength, don't suggest difficult tasks that he can't do. If he thinks his own decisions are brave, don't point out they may be unlawful. That would anger him. If he thinks he has a smart plan, don't mention past failures. In this way you can become near and dear to him, avoid all suspicion, and use your speech to accomplish things.

9. Can Lying Be Justified?
A Case Study in Medical Ethics

A sixty-nine year old man had a routine physical examination in preparation for a short vacation in Australia. The doctor suspected a serious problem and ordered more testing. The results showed that the man had incurable cancer of the prostate gland. The tumor was very small and very slow-growing. The doctor knew that as the tumor got bigger there were good treatments for relieving pain and discomfort.

The doctor had treated this patient over many years and knew him very well. Although the man was intelligent, had a good job, and was able to take care of himself, he also suffered from depression. This man had no living relatives except his children with whom he had quarreled and who had nothing to do with him. A short time before, his wife had died and he had tried to commit suicide. This trip to Australia was the first thing he had become excited about for years.

The patient also was known to become very depressed when informed about health problems. He worried too much and became incapable of thinking clearly. The doctor believed that telling him about his cancer would bring on severe depression and irrational behavior.

When the tests were complete and the patient returned to the doctor to learn the results he asked the doctor nervously, "Am I okay?" Without waiting for an answer, he asked, "I don't have cancer, do I?" Believing that the patient would not experience any symptoms from the cancer during the trip to Australia, the doctor said, "You are as good as you were ten years ago." He worried about telling such a lie but firmly believed it was the right thing to do.

10. *Boy and Mt. Fuji*
by **Katsushika Hokusai**

and

A Photograph of Mt. Fuji

(Turn to the end of the book for these reproductions.)

11. *The Lives of Greeks and Romans* by **Plutarch**

Life of Cato, The Younger

Cato came from a very famous family. Even as a child he didn't laugh and cry very much. His face and his speech didn't show how he felt. Unlike other children, he stuck with whatever project he started and carried it through. He was rough toward people who tried to flatter him, and paid no attention to those who threatened him. It was hard to make him laugh. It was also hard to make him angry. But once he got angry, he did not calm down very easily.

When he first went to school he showed that he was slow at learning things. But once he did learn something, he never forgot it. This is the way things are naturally. Some students learn quickly, can give answers back quickly, but just as quickly forget what they have learned. However, people who learn with pain and difficulty remember best, since everything they learn is burnt in their minds. It doesn't fade quickly.

Cato was stubborn and did not very easily believe what

other people told him. These qualities made him a difficult student. This is because learning requires that you allow someone, your teacher, to persuade you of something. People who are stubborn are hard to persuade of anything. Those who are easy to persuade lack a certain kind of strength. For this reason, young people are easier to persuade than older people and therefore they are better students. Sick people are easier to persuade than healthy people—they are hoping to be cured.

Although Cato was hard to teach, he was not disobedient. He would do whatever his teacher asked. But he never took anything at face value. He always asked, "Why?"

One day, when he was still a child, a famous politician came to visit his father and uncle. As a joke the politician asked Cato and his brother to put in a good word for him with their father and uncle. Cato's brother smiled and said, "Yes." However, Cato looked at him steadily and angrily. Then the politician asked Cato himself, "And you, young sir, what do you say to us? Will you, as well as your brother, put in a good word for us with your uncle?" Cato continued to give no answer, in this way making it clear that he wouldn't do what the politician asked. The politician then pretended to get angry, picked Cato up, and held him out a window as if to drop him. He asked Cato again if he would put in a good word. Cato remained silent. The man then put him down and said, "What a blessing that he is a child. If he were a man, we wouldn't get one vote from the people."

12. *Society in America*
by Harriet Martineau

    The great and ruling idea of American government is that the majority is right. However, often what the majority actually decides does not quite agree with this idea. One reason for this is that for a majority of the people to learn by experience is slow work. It may be sure but it is slow. So it often happens that a few sensible men are sooner in the right than the majority on particular issues. It therefore requires great patience and faith on the part of these few men. They are in advance of the majority on particular points and could carry the nation forward if they didn't have to wait for the majority. The majority eventually chooses the best course of action, but this can take a long time filled with mistakes and failures as the people learn from experience.

    The great idea also holds that the majority will choose the best leaders. This is even further from being true in practice. The best leaders in America have in fact often been men who disagreed with the majority on both general issues of government and on particular policies. This raises a serious question. Is a better and honest man who disagrees with the majority a more dangerous ruler than a worse and perhaps dishonest man who agrees with it?

There are two grounds of hope in America. The first is that Americans live out the saying, 'What is everybody's business is nobody's business.' No one stirs against an abuse that is no more his than anyone else's. The abuse continues until it finally threatens law and freedom. Then the majority rises up and crushes it. This has happened many times and we can hope that when these problems get even worse, the majority will suddenly respond and cure them.

The other hope is in the political imagination of the Americans. Their fathers in the founding of the country did a deed which the world had never seen before, and their children have not yet forgotten that success. These Americans are like a great young poet—now moody, now wild but bringing forth works of absolute sense. They have caught the truth of the past, have looked into the future, and will create something so magnificent as the world can scarcely begin to dream of. There is great hope in a nation that is able to be possessed by an idea. And this ability has been the special characteristic of Americans from their first day as a country until now.

13. *Fire and Ice*
by Robert Frost

Some say the world will end in fire,
Some say ice.
From what I've tasted of desire
I hold with those who favor fire.
But if it had to perish twice,
I think I know enough of hate
To say that for destruction ice
Is also great
And would suffice.

14. *The Confessions* by St. Augustine

What is time? I know what time is when no one asks me. But when someone does ask and I try to explain it, I find I get confused and do not know. At least I feel sure about saying that if nothing passed away, there would be no past, and if nothing were coming, there would be no future; and if nothing were now, there would be no present. But how can we say that the past and the future *are*. The past no longer is and the future is not yet. But if the present were always present and didn't go into the past, we would not have time at all. We would have an everlasting present and that is what we mean by eternity.

If the future and past exist, I want to know where they are. Wherever they are, they cannot be there as future and past. They would have to be there as present. For if they are future, they are not yet there. And if they are past, they are no longer there. Thus, wherever they are, and whatever they are, they cannot be anything except present. But where are they?

It must be clear that neither the future nor the past exists. It is incorrect to say there are three times—past, present, and future. There is only one time and we call it the present. One might say instead, "Yes, there are three times—a present of things past, a present of things present, and a present of things future." But again where are these three present times? The only place where I can find them is in our own minds. The present of things past is memory. The present of things present is sight and feeling. The present of things future is hope and expectation.

If we are allowed to use words in this way, then I say there are three times. I am willing to say, "There are three times—past, present and future." It is an incorrect way to use language, but it is our custom to speak that way. I do not mind. I do not object as long as we understand what we are saying. And what we are saying is that neither what is future nor what is past is now in existence. We do not often use language correctly. Usually we use it incorrectly, though we understand one another.

15. On National Education
by Mary Wollstonecraft

When children spend most of their time with adults, they soon get a kind of early maturity which often stops the growth of their minds. In order to develop their abilities, they should be encouraged to think for themselves. This can only happen by mixing children together and making them jointly go after the same objects. Children get very lazy when, instead of seeking out answers and information for themselves, they spend most of their time asking adults questions and relying on the information they receive. When this happens, the child's abilities are often harmed because they are brought forward too quickly. And this will happen if children spend most of their time with adults, however wise and thoughtful the adults may be. With their equals in age, this could never happen. The subjects of inquiry, though adults might influence them, would not be entirely directed.

Besides, the seeds of their future feelings are sown in childhood. The respect which is felt for a parent or an adult is very different from the social feelings that will form their future happiness. This is based on equality and it results from feeling untroubled by an adult's observing them in a serious manner, which often prevents arguments and conflicts. However much children respect their parents, they will always want to play and talk with others of their own age. The very respect children feel for parents is mixed with some fear. This will prevent them from pouring out the little secrets which first open their hearts to friendship and confidence. These feelings will later lead them to generosity. In addition, they will never gain that frank openness of behavior which young people can only attain by being frequently with others with whom they dare to speak what they think. This only happens with other young people. With adults and their parents, they are often afraid of being criticized for thinking they know things they may not or being laughed at for being foolish.

16. *The Autobiography*
by Charles Darwin

I have said that in one respect my mind has changed during the last twenty or thirty years. Up to the age of thirty or beyond, poetry of many kinds gave me great pleasure. Even as a school-boy I took great delight in Shakespeare, especially in the historical plays. Paintings and especially music also used to give me great delight. But for many years now I cannot stand to read poetry. I have tried recently to read Shakespeare, and found it so dull that it sickened me. I have also almost lost any taste for paintings or music. Music mostly sets me thinking on what I have been working on instead of giving me pleasure. I retain some taste for fine scenery, but it does not please me as much as it used to.

On the other hand, novels have, for many years, been a wonderful relief and pleasure to me. I often bless all novelists. I like novels that have happy endings. I think a law ought to be passed against novels with unhappy endings. A novel, according to my taste, is not first-class unless it contains a person you can thoroughly love. If it is a pretty woman, all the better.

This peculiar and regrettable loss of taste for the arts is very odd since books on history, travel, biographies, and essays on all sorts of subjects interest me as much as they ever did.

My mind seems to have become a kind of machine for grinding general laws out of large collections of facts. Why this should have resulted in the weakening of that part of the brain on which a taste for the arts depends I don't understand. A man with a stronger and better organized mind would not have suffered the same loss I suppose. If I had my life to live again I would have made a rule to read some poetry and listen to some music at least once a week. Perhaps the part of my brain responsible for a taste for the arts would not have become weakened. The loss of these tastes is a loss of happiness. The intellect may also be injured by this loss, and more probably our moral character, because the emotional part of our nature has also been weakened.

17. *On Nature*
by Lucretius

The universe has no boundary or end in any direction. For, if there were a limit to the universe, some part of it would be the outermost edge. But isn't it obvious that nothing has an outermost edge unless there is something else beyond it which lets us see that it ends and makes it clear to us why our senses, for example our eyesight, can see no farther? Since we must agree that there is nothing external and outside the whole universe, the entire universe does not have such an outermost edge. It therefore does not have an end or limit. It makes no difference where in the universe you stand, the universe extends equally without limit in every direction. But let us pretend that the universe has a limit. Suppose that a man goes to the very edge of the universe, to the very outermost boundary or place, and hurls a spear. What will happen to such a spear hurled with great force? Either it will go in the direction he threw it and fly farther, or something will stand in its way and stop it. You must accept one of these two alternatives. But both of them cut off all escape and force you to admit that the universe goes on without any end to it. For if something stops the spear from going forward and reaching its target, then the spear was not, as we supposed, thrown from the extreme edge. For what stopped it was really the extreme edge. We must therefore carry the spear to this new place and try again. In the other case, where the spear does in fact fly forward, it is clear that it was not originally thrown from the extreme edge. And we can continue this argument. Wherever you place the edge or outermost boundary of the universe, I ask you what happens in the case of the spear. The result is that a boundary for the entire universe can be fixed nowhere and that the spear will always be able to fly farther.

18. *Gorgias*
by Plato

Callicles: Now I'm going to tell you, Socrates, what justice really is. Nature shows us that it is only just and proper that the stronger person should lord over the weaker. Nature shows us everywhere that this is the true state of affairs, not only among animals, but also among countries, states, and all groups of people. This is, in fact, how justice works: the stronger shall rule and take advantage over the weaker. By what principle of justice did King Xerxes invade Greece? Because he was strong: and there are many, many similar examples.

To my mind, men are acting by *natural justice* when they behave like that.

But weak people (that is, the majority of humans) get together and try to make laws to tame everyone, including the strong. It's just like we do when we try to tame wild animals—to make them do as they are told. We call them *state laws, civil laws,* or *human laws.* But if a man has sufficient strength, he will trample those laws and rules underfoot. He will stand out as our master, and the justice of nature will shine out.

Socrates: Tell me Callicles, is it those who are physically more powerful that you call stronger, and must the weaker obey the stronger? You seemed to state that when you said that great nations attack small ones in accordance with natural justice. So do you claim that "stronger" and "better" are one and the same thing?

Callicles: I assure you they are the same.

Socrates: But isn't the majority always more powerful than any one person? Since it is, the laws of the majority are laws made by the stronger. And therefore it is by natural justice that the strong individual is tamed by the laws of the majority, but this is exactly the opposite of what you claimed. What do you mean Callicles? Tell us who or what you mean by stronger. You can't simply mean physically stronger.

Callicles: This is what I mean. Natural justice is that the better and wiser man should rule over and have more than the inferior.

19. *Letter to Her Mother*
by Amandine Dupin (George Sand)

31 May 1831

My dear Mother,

I know you're not feeling very cheerful, are you, because you are going to be alone. However, friendship and companionship are very difficult to combine with freedom. You like having people with you but, just like me, you hate any kind of limit to your freedom. How does one ever balance one's own desires with those of other people? I really don't know. For me, freedom of thought and action is the greatest blessing. I wish one could combine them with the little cares and pleasures of raising a family. That would be sweet, but is it really possible? The one always seems to get in the way of the other. Freedom interferes with one's family and friends, and they interfere with it. You alone can judge which you would prefer to give up.

For myself, I know my greatest fault is that I can't endure the least shadow of force or pressure. Whatever is imposed on me as a duty becomes difficult and intolerable. Whatever I do of my own free will I do with all my heart. I think it's a great misfortune to be made this way and this is the origin of all my failings toward other people. But can you change your own nature? When people are indulgent or relaxed about this fault of mine, it corrects itself in the most wonderful way. But when I am blamed and criticized for it, it gets much worse. That is not because I want to be difficult. It is just involuntary. I can't resist it. You think I love pleasure and need amusement. It isn't people and noise and theaters and clothing I want. You're the only one who thinks that of me. It's freedom I want. I want to be able to walk out quite alone and say to myself, "I will eat dinner at four or at seven, just as I like. I'll go to the park by walking up one street rather than another quite as the whim seizes me." That would please me much more than going to parties and spending time with people as you imagine about me. Why do people have this incredible desire to torment each other? Why do we blame one another's faults? Why do we show no pity to anyone who is not made just like us?

Write soon, My dear Mother,

Amandine

20. *The Autobiography of Malcolm X*
by Malcolm X

Many who today hear me somewhere in person, or on television, or those who read something I've said, will think I went to school far beyond the eighth grade. This impression is due entirely to my studies in prison.

It had really begun back in the Charlestown Prison, when Bimbi first made me feel envy of his stock of knowledge. Bimbi had always taken charge of any conversation he was in, and I had tried to emulate him. But every book I picked up had few sentences which didn't contain anywhere from one to nearly all of the words that might as well have been Chinese. When I just skipped those words, of course, I really ended up with little idea of what the book said. So I had come to the Norfolk Prison Colony still going through only book-reading motions. Pretty soon, I would have quit even these motions, unless I had received the motivation that I did.

I saw that the best thing I could do was get hold of a dictionary—to study, to learn some words. I was lucky enough to reason also that I should try to improve my penmanship. It was sad. I couldn't even write in a straight line. It was both ideas together that moved me to request a dictionary along with some tablets and pencils from the Norfolk Prison Colony School.

I spent two days just riffling uncertainly through the dictionary pages. I'd never realized so many words existed! I didn't know *which* words I needed to learn. Finally, just to start some kind of action, I began copying.

In my slow, painstaking, ragged handwriting, I copied into my tablet everything printed on that first page, down to the punctuation marks.

I believe it took me a day. Then, aloud, I read back, to myself, everything I'd written on the tablet. Over and over, aloud, to myself, I read my own handwriting.

I woke up the next morning, thinking about those words—immensely proud to realize that not only had I written so much at one time, but I'd written words that I never knew were in the world. Moreover, with a little effort, I also could remember what many of these words meant. I reviewed the words whose meanings I didn't remember.

I was so fascinated that I went on—I copied the dictionary's next page. And the same experience came when

I studied that. With every succeeding page, I also learned of people and places and events from history. Actually the dictionary is like a miniature encyclopedia. Finally the dictionary's A section had filled a whole tablet—and I went on into the B's. That was the way I started copying what eventually became the entire dictionary.

I suppose it was inevitable that as my word-base broadened, I could for the first time pick up a book and read and now begin to understand what the book was saying. Anyone who has read a great deal can imagine the new world that opened. Let me tell you something: from then until I left that prison, in every free moment I had, if I was not reading in the library, I was reading on my bunk. In fact, up to then, I never had been so truly free in my life.

21. *Discourse on Method*
by René Descartes

Common sense is the most fairly distributed thing in the world because everyone believes he has enough of it. Even people who are very hard to please in everything else usually do not want more of it than what they already have. It is not likely that everyone is mistaken in this matter. Rather, it shows that the power to judge correctly and to distinguish the true from the false is naturally equal in all human beings. This power is, in fact, what we mean by common sense, or *reason*. Hence, the diversity of our opinions does not arise because some of us are more reasonable than others. Rather, this diversity arises because we direct our thoughts along different paths and think about different things. For it is not enough to have a good mind. The main thing is to use it correctly. The greatest minds are capable of great evil as well as great good. Those who walk very slowly go ahead much farther if they always follow that right path than those who run but stray from the right path.

As for me, I have never thought that my mind is more perfect than that of most human beings. I have even often wished that my mind were as quick, or my imagination as clear, or my memory as good as those of some other people. For apart from these things, I know no other qualities which perfect our minds. As for common sense, or *reason*, I prefer to believe that every human being has as much of it as any other, since it is what makes us human beings and distinguishes us from the other animals.

22. *On Arguments*
by Chuang Tzu

1. Let's suppose that you and I have just had an argument. One of us might have won. If you won and I lost, does that mean that you are right and I am wrong? Or if I had beaten you in the argument instead of your beating me, would that show that I was right and you were wrong? Is it necessary that one of us was right and the other was wrong? Or isn't it possible that both of us were right or both of us were wrong? Perhaps we could find someone to help us decide. But since you and I don't know who was right, why should others know any better? And anyway, whom would we choose to help us decide who was right? Should we get someone who agrees with you? But if he agrees with you, how can he decide fairly? Shall we get someone who agrees with me? But if he already agrees with me, how can he decide between us? Perhaps we should find someone who disagrees with both of us. But then neither of us would choose him, since we will both disagree with him. Or should we find someone who agrees with both of us? But if we could, why were we arguing in the first place? Clearly then neither arguing

between ourselves nor consulting other people can help us decide who was right.

2. Once Chuang Chou dreamt he was a butterfly, a butterfly fluttering from flower to flower in the sunshine, happy with himself and doing just as he pleased. He didn't know he was Chuang Chou. Suddenly he woke up and there he was—Chuang Chou. But he didn't know if he was Chuang Chou who had dreamt he was a butterfly or a butterfly dreaming he was Chuang Chou. Surely between a butterfly and Chuang Chou there must be some difference.

23. *On Laziness*
by Michel de Montaigne

When I retired recently, my only thought was to bother about nothing but spending the little life I had left alone and in peace. It seemed to me that I could do my mind no greater favor than to leave it alone with no work to do but think about itself. I hoped it could do this more easily now that I had become wiser and more self-sufficient with time. But I find that my mind gives itself a hundred times more trouble than it had when I was busy. It gives birth to many fantastic monsters one after another without order or purpose. I have recently decided, in order to think about this experience, to put these monsters down in writing. I hope in time to make my mind ashamed of itself for its laziness.

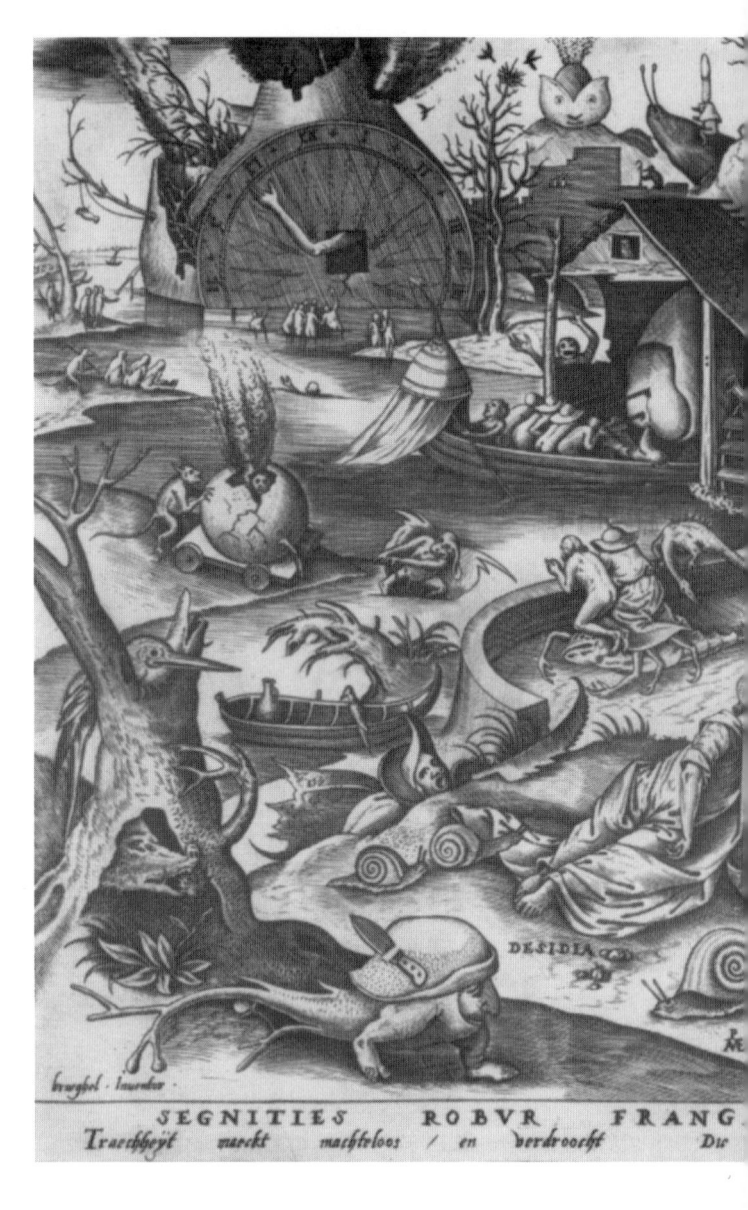

Sloth; Pieter BRUEGEL, the Elder *from* The Seven C<
Rosenwald Collection (Date: 1558; Engraving)

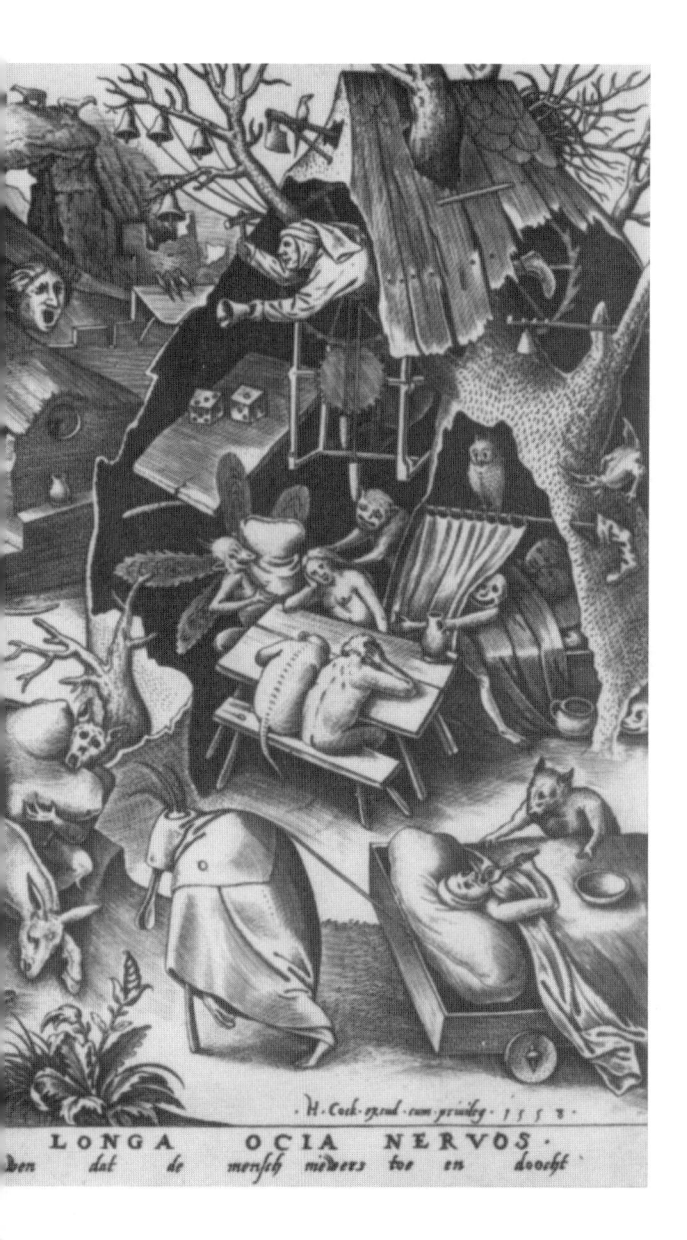

LONGA OCIA NERVOS.
ben dat de menfch nievers toe en dooght

Sins; National Gallery of Art, Washington, D.C.;

24. *The Way of Righteousness*
The Sayings of Buddha

1. All that we are is the result of what we have thought: it is founded on our thoughts, it is made up of our thoughts. If a man speaks or acts with an evil thought, pain follows him, as the wheel follows the foot of the ox that draws the carriage.

2. All that we are is the result of what we have thought: it is founded on our thoughts, it is made up of our thoughts. If a man speaks or acts with a pure thought, happiness follows him like a shadow that never leaves him.

3. "He abused me, he beat me, he defeated me, he robbed me"—in those who harbor such thoughts hatred will never cease.

4. "He abused me, he beat me, he defeated me, he robbed me"—in those who do not harbor such thoughts hatred will cease.

5. For hatred does not cease by hatred at any time: hatred ceases by love—this is an old rule.

6. The world does not know that we must all come to an end here; but for those who know it, their quarrels cease at once.

7. He who lives looking for pleasures only—his senses uncontrolled, eating and drinking too much, idle and weak—will certainly be destroyed, as the wind destroys a weak tree.

8. They who imagine truth in untruth and see untruth in truth, never arrive at truth, but follow useless desires.

9. They who know truth in truth, and untruth in untruth, arrive at truth, and follow true desires.

10. As rain breaks through an ill-thatched house, passion will break through an unreflecting mind.

11. As rain does not break through a well-built house, passion will not break through a well-reflecting mind.

12. The evil-doer mourns in this world, and he mourns in the next; he mourns in both. He mourns and suffers when he sees the evil result of his own work.

13. The good man delights in this world, and he delights in the next; he delights in both. He delights and rejoices when he sees the purity of his own work.

14. The evil-doer suffers in this world, and he suffers in the next; he suffers in both. He suffers when he thinks of the evil he has done, he suffers more when going on the evil path.

15. The thoughtless man—even if he can recite a large portion of the law but is not a doer of it—has no share in ruling, but is like a cowherd counting the cows of others.

16. The doer of the law, even if he can recite only a small portion of the law, has indeed a share in the ruling. This is because he has given up passion and hatred and foolishness. He possesses true knowledge and peace of mind because he cares for nothing in this world or the world to come.

25. Selected Articles from the U.S. and U.S.S.R. Constitutions

U.S.
The Amendments

Article One—*Freedom of Religion, of Speech, and of the Press:*

Congress shall make no law respecting the establishment of religion, or prohibiting the free exercise thereof; or abridging the freedom of speech, or of the press; or the right of the people peaceably to assemble, and to petition the government for a redress of grievances.

Article Five—*Rights of an Accused Person:*

No person...shall be compelled in any criminal case to be a witness against himself, nor be deprived of life, liberty, or property, without due process of law.

Article Thirteen—*Abolition of Slavery:*

Neither slavery nor involuntary servitude, except as a punishment for crime, whereof the party shall have been duly convicted, shall exist within the United States, or any place subject to their jurisdiction.

Article Fifteen—*Equal Rights for All Citizens:*

The right of citizens of the United States to vote shall not be denied or abridged by the United States or by any state on account of race, color, or previous condition of servitude.

Article Sixteen—*Authorizing Income Taxes:*

The Congress shall have power to lay and collect taxes on incomes, from whatever source derived, ...

Article Nineteen—*Women can Vote:*

The right of citizens of the United States to vote shall not be denied or abridged by the United States or by any state on account of sex.

Selected Articles from the Constitution of the U.S.S.R.

Article 118 Citizens of the USSR are guaranteed the right to work and to be paid in accordance with the amount and kind of such work.

Article 119 Citizens of the USSR have the right to rest and leisure. This is ensured by establishing an 8-hour workday for office employees, a 7 or 6-hour workday for more strenuous jobs, and a 4-hour workday for work in factories. Full pay is guaranteed for all who work, plus annual vacations and a wide network of rest homes, resorts and clubs to serve the working people.

Article 120 Citizens of the USSR have the right to free medical service for the working people, and social insurance will be given to workers in their old age.

Article 121 Citizens of the USSR have the right to free education for 7 years for all students; for advanced schooling for outstanding students; and for vocational, technical, and farm training as appropriate. All education is to be free; no payment is permitted.

Article 122 Women in the USSR are accorded equal rights with men in all spheres of economic, state, cultural, social and political life. These rights are ensured by granting women an equal right to work, payment for work, rest and leisure, old age insurance, education, state protection of the interests of mother and child, state aid to mothers of large families and unmarried mothers, natal care, and maternity leave with full pay and free kindergartens.

26. *The Groom's Crimes*
A Tale from China

Lord Ching was once the ruler of a large area in China. He had a horse he loved. The animal was so important to him that when his country went to war he entrusted the care of this horse to a particular person in his palace. This man was to do nothing else but look after the king's horse. However, the horse died suddenly and Ching became furious. He had his men seize his servant and ordered his soldiers to cut off the man's arms and legs.

At this time it happened that Yen Tzu, one of the wisest men in China, was visiting this king. When the king's soldiers entered with the man and took out their swords, the wise man stepped in front of the king. "My Lord, long ago there were great emperors who ruled in China. These men ruled only by the example they gave to their subjects. If one of their people were to have their limbs cut off, with whose arms and legs do you think they would start?" "With the king's own arms and legs," said King Ching. Understanding the wise man's point, he canceled the punishment and gave orders to have the man executed by the normal methods employed at that time.

However, the wise man Yen Tzu interrupted again. "If you hang him, he will die ignorant of his crimes. Why don't I explain his crimes to him before he dies so he will not imagine he is being treated unfairly?"

"Very well," said King Ching.

The wise man approached the prisoner and in a loud voice said, "You have committed three crimes. You were told to care for the horse and instead, you let it die. That's one crime for which you deserve death. Secondly, the horse was the King's favorite and because of you, he has become sad. That's another crime for which you deserve to die. But thirdly and most importantly, you caused the king to put a man to death for the sake of a mere animal. When the people learn about it, they will hate our king. When other kings learn about it, they will despise our state. So by neglecting our king's horse, you have created trouble among our people and made us look ridiculous to our neighbors. For all these reasons you deserve to die." The prisoner held his head in his hands as he heard his crimes. The king however gave a deep sigh. "Free the man," he said. "Set him free or my honor and reputation will be ruined."

27. *The Stonecutter*
A Tale from Japan

A long time ago there lived a stonecutter. Everyday he went to a mountain to cut slabs for tombstones. He was contented and asked for nothing he didn't have. One day, delivering a tombstone to the home of a rich merchant, he saw beautiful things and treasures. He suddenly longed for silk curtains and fine furniture and sighed, "If only I were rich." The voice of a mountain spirit heard him and said, "Your wish is heard." Confused, the man went home and found a large home filled with just the treasures he wanted. He lived this way in great joy until summer.

That summer, the air was hot. He couldn't breath and he often found he was bored. So he looked out the window. There he saw a beautiful horse-drawn carriage with servants who fanned and amused a prince. "If only I were a prince!" he said. The mountain voice heard—"You shall be a prince," was the reply. Suddenly he was in a carriage, fanned and amused by servants. For a while he was thrilled, but he soon noticed at his palace that though servants poured water on his grass the sun burned it and he sweated at night even though he was fanned. "The sun is mightier than I am," he sighed. "I wish I were the sun." Again the spirit heard and gave him his wish. Now he felt proud of his power. He flashed his light on everyone, burned up grass fields, and made princes and stonecutters sweat. But one day he became sad. There was nothing left for him to do and when a cloud passed between him and the earth, he became upset. "The cloud holds me a prisoner. It captures my rays and light. It is mightier than I am. If only I were a cloud." In a moment, he became a cloud thanks to the mountain spirit. Now he floated between the sun and the earth. Sometimes he let the sunlight through, sometimes the rain. Because of him the fields grew green and rice grew in the rice paddies. One day, to test his power, he sent rain. It rained for weeks. Cities were destroyed, floods were everywhere. Only a great rock on the mountainside remained. "Is this rock mightier than I am? If only I were a rock." Once more the mountain spirit gave him his wish. As a rock, he gloried in his power. Neither sun nor rain could move him. "Finally, I am the most powerful of all," he said, looking forward to contentment. However, even as he felt this joy he heard a strange sound at his feet. He faintly remembered such a sound but couldn't identify it. He looked down from his great height and saw a stonecutter cutting into his surface. As he watched, a trembling feeling ran through him, and a great slab broke off and fell to the ground. Furious, he screamed, "Can a mere stonecutter be mightier than a massive mountain? If only I were a stonecutter!" And immediately he became a man again. He worked, he was poor, he sweated, and he learned to cut stones again. But he didn't long to be somebody else any more, to hunger for what he didn't have, or to be more powerful. Finally he had learned to be happy.

28. The Pillow Book
by Sei Shonagon

143. *Feeling that One is Disliked by Others*

Feeling that one is disliked by others is surely one of the saddest things in the world. No one, however foolish, could wish such a thing on himself. Yet everywhere, whether it be in the Palace or at home with one's family, there are some people who are naturally liked and others who are not.

Not only among people of good birth, where it goes without saying, but even among commoners, children are adored by their parents. This naturally attracts the attention of strangers, and everyone makes a great fuss over them. If they are attractive children, it is only natural that their parents should dote on them. How could it be otherwise? But, if the children have nothing particular to recommend them, one can only assume that such devotion comes merely from the fact of being parents.

I imagine that there can be nothing so delightful as to be loved by everyone—one's parents, one's teacher, and all the people with whom one is on close terms.

145. *Sympathy is the Most Splendid of All Qualities*

Sympathy is the most splendid of all qualities. This is especially true when it is found in men, but it also applies to women. Compassionate remarks of the type, "How sad for you!" (to someone who has suffered a misfortune) or, "I can imagine what he must be feeling!" (said about a man who has had some sorrow) are bound to give pleasure, however casual such a remark may be. If one's remark is addressed to someone else and repeated to the sufferer, it is even more effective than if one makes it directly. The unhappy person will never forget such a kindness and will be anxious to let one know how it has moved him.

If it is someone who is close to one and who expects sympathetic inquiries, he will not be especially pleased, since he is merely getting what he expects. But a friendly remark passed on to people whom we are less close to is certain to give pleasure. This all sounds simple enough, yet hardly anyone seems to bother. Altogether it seems as if men and women with good heads rarely have good hearts. Yet I suppose there must be some who are both clever and kind.

146. *It is Absurd for People to Get Angry*

It is absurd for people to get angry because someone else has gossiped about them. How can anyone be so simple as to believe that he is free to find fault with others while his own faults are passed over in silence? Yet when someone hears that he has been discussed unfavorably he is always outraged, and this I find most unattractive.

If I am really close to someone, I realize that it would be hurtful to speak badly about him. When the opportunity for gossip arises, I hold my peace. In all other cases, however, I freely speak my mind and make everyone laugh.

29. The Most Frugal Man in the World
A Tale from China

Liang spent very little money—only what he needed to eat. And he used no more of his goods than he thought absolutely necessary. In other words, he was what we call "very frugal." One day he heard about a man who was even more careful with his property than himself. A traveler told him that this other man was the most frugal man in the whole world. Since Liang wanted his son to become even more frugal than himself, he hoped his son could take lessons from this great master. However, an exchange of gifts was needed to make contact, and Liang thought long and hard about what to send. Finally he decided on the proper gift. He gave his son the smallest coin there was—a penny—and told him to go and buy the very cheapest brown paper. When his son came back, Liang cut up the paper into small pieces. On one, he drew the head of a pig. Placing the drawing in a ceremonial gift basket he sent his son off to visit the master of frugality.

When Liang's son arrived at the great master's home, the master's son greeted him. Liang's son explained why he had come and presented the gift. The master's son, on seeing the drawing said, "We have nothing in the house worthy to take the place of the pig's head in your basket. But to show we gratefully received your gift, I will send back an orange." The master's son, using one of his hands formed the shape of an orange with his fingers and then carefully placed it in the basket. Liang's son returned home eager to tell his father about a level of thrift surpassing even theirs.

Soon after Liang's son left, the great master came out of his house and his son told him of Liang's gift. "And what did you send back in return?" the master asked his son. "I formed an orange with my right hand and placed it carefully in the basket," said his son, demonstrating what he had done. The master became furious. He seized his son and hit him. "You wasteful wretch," he said. "Your fingers were spread too far apart. The orange you formed would appear much too large. And what is worse, you didn't have to tell me what you did as well as demonstrate it for me."

30. *A Philosophical Essay on Probabilities*
by Pierre Simon, Marquis de Laplace

There are illusions of mind, just as there are illusions of sight. And just as the sense of touch corrects illusions of sight, careful thinking corrects illusions of the mind. Our passions, prejudices, and opinions are sources of dangerous illusions. They do this by exaggerating the probabilities favorable to them and paying no attention to the probabilities against them.

It is primarily in gambling that illusions make us hopeful of winning in spite of having very little chance of winning in reality. Most people who play in the lotteries do not know the odds in their favor and the odds against them. They see only the possibility of winning a lot of money with a small stake. The chance of winning a lot of money makes them exaggerate the possibility of actually winning. Poor people, excited by the desire to improve their lives, risk much needed money on bets that have very little chance of winning. People would be astonished at how little chance they have of winning the lottery. However, the authorities take great care to publicize the winners not the losers.

In addition, when a number in the lottery has not been drawn for a long time, the crowd is eager to bet on it. They think that since the number has not been drawn for a long time the chances of it being drawn have increased. This error is caused by an illusion which makes us think that the past always influences the present. It is, for example, very unlikely that you will throw ten heads in a row in flipping coins. This leads us to believe that if heads has been thrown nine times, than the chance of tails coming up the tenth time has increased. But it has not. The chance is still one in two. A similar illusion persuades people that they can win in the lottery by betting on the same number every time until the number comes up.

The theory of probability teaches us to distrust our first opinions. As we recognize that our first opinions often deceive us, we ought to conclude that we should trust them only after we have tested them thoroughly.

Mt. Fuji Reproductions

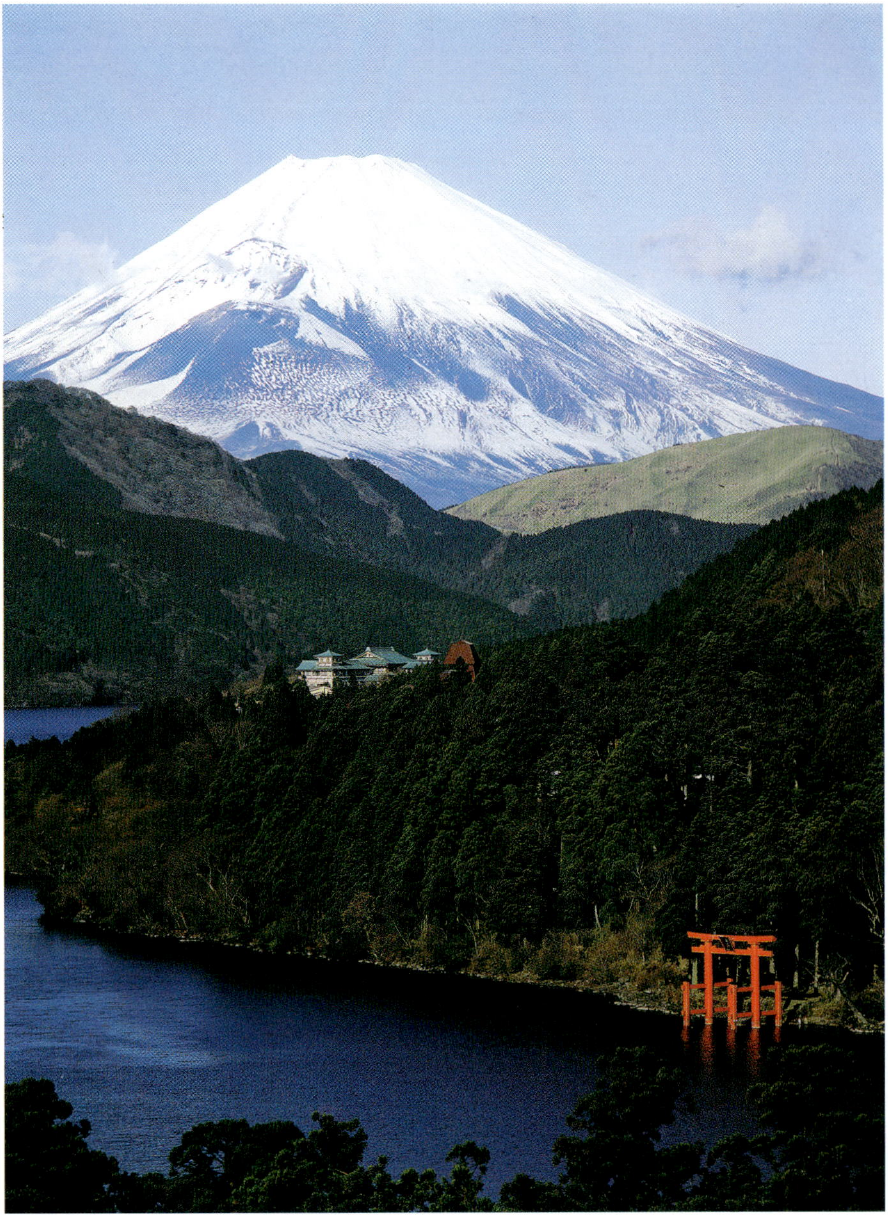